THE CAPE COD COTTAGE

THE CAPE COD COTTAGE

WILLIAM MORGAN

FOREWORD BY DANIEL V. SCULLY

PRINCETON ARCHITECTURAL PRESS, NEW YORK

TO CAROLYN

Published by
Princeton Architectural Press
37 East Seventh Street
New York, New York 10003

For a free catalog of books, call 1.800.722.6657.
Visit our web site at www.papress.com.

Publication of this book has been supported by a grant
from the Graham Foundation for Advanced Studies in
the Fine Arts.

Editing: Jennifer N. Thompson
Design: Deb Wood

Special thanks to: Nettie Aljian, Dorothy Ball, Nicola Bednarek, Janet Behning,
Megan Carey, Penny (Yuen Pik) Chu, Russell Fernandez, Jan Haux, Clare
Jacobson, John King, Mark Lamster, Nancy Eklund Later, Linda Lee, Katharine
Myers, Lauren Nelson, Scott Tennent, Paul Wagner, and Joe Weston of
Princeton Architectural Press —Kevin C. Lippert, publisher

Library of Congress Cataloging-in-Publication Data

Morgan, William, 1944–
  The Cape Cod cottage / William Morgan ; foreword by Daniel V. Scully.
      p. cm.
  Includes bibliographical references.
  ISBN-13: 978-1-56898-575-6 (pbk. : alk. paper)
  1. Cape Cod houses. 2. Architecture, Domestic—United States. 3.
Architecture, Domestic—Massachusetts—Cape Cod. I. Title.
  NA7205.M6794 2006
  728'.370974492—dc22
                                        2005026158

Cover images by Will Morgan
Front cover: Chatham, Massachusetts
Back cover, left: Eastham, Massachusetts
Back cover, right: Mattapoisett, Massachusetts

CONTENTS

ACKNOWLEDGMENTS

The Graham Foundation for Advanced Studies in the
Fine Arts provided the grant that transformed an interest
in Cape Cod cottages into this study.

Many people contributed to this book. Whitney Morrill created
the drawings, while Traer Scott printed the photographs.
Ned Pratt and William Richards helped with research.

Preservationists and architects among them Earle Shettleworth,
Christi Mitchell, William McKenzie Woodward, James Garvin,
Jayne Merkel, Elizabeth Padjen, and Grattan Gill shared
knowledge, experience, and advice. Homeowners were both
generous and enthusiastic.

Princeton Architectural Press's Kevin Lippert and
Jennifer Thompson's belief in the project has, I hope,
not been misplaced.

My wife Carolyn was my constant muse; the book is as
much hers as mine.

FOREWORD

In New England we do not do Capes anymore. The decently small house, inward-directed, cohesive, and self-contained, seems to have been eclipsed by the ranch house as the "starter" home.

The Cape is such a simple and direct plan—a central door, hall and stairs, with rooms off to each side. Each room is foursquare with windows on two or three sides. What more do you want? On the second floor there is a bath at the top of stairs and a bedroom off to each side. Windows are located on the side gables, and sometimes dormers give a second source of light and cross ventilation. The form is direct and honest; it cannot be made more modest or quietly symmetrical. With a central front door, there is pride of place. The image still works, but today the door is a formality, one-upped by the attached garage.

Appearing as a small one story with the second floor tucked up under a decent roof pitch, the Cape is not about strutting one's size. No wonder this English form sprouted so well in the New England soil and climate. Perhaps puritanically the Cape exposes such minimal skin that it appears stingy to our super-sized culture.

Lining the street, each with a walkway leading from the sidewalk to the front door, Capes can cumulatively make a community. The current domestic shapes of narcissism, with only a driveway leading to the street, are more about self than community.

Is it just easier to add a side door or garage to a ranch house? Or is the shape of a Cape just not self-congratulatory enough? Or is it now required that each kid get a room? Has the focus on the warm central hearth been replaced by the cool glow of the worldwide web? Or have we been sold a bill of "gotta-have-a great-room" goods? Architectural clients come bearing their antique Cape with pride, and then want to add a great room, a great kitchen, great closets, and great baths. Pretty soon the Cape is not so great anymore. The contradictions abound. If and when what "I need and I want" gives way to what we really need, perhaps the Cape will make a comeback.

Daniel V. Scully

Eastham, Massachusetts, Governor Thomas Prence house, 1646
(photographed pre-1880)

ESSAY

A child's first drawing of a house is essentially a Cape Cod: a story-and-a-half, gable roof, big chimney emitting welcoming smoke. Ask someone to describe a Cape and invariably they use words like "small," "sheltering," and "cozy." Narrow windows, a central chimney, rose bushes and lilacs, maybe a picket fence and the Stars and Stripes fill out the picture.

The Cape Cod cottage is the nearly perfect house. A combination of necessity and tradition, the Cape Cod has been a fundamental, iconic, and enduring expression of the American home for almost four hundred years. The humble and ubiquitous Cape has endured from its development by yeoman English settlers along the shores of Massachusetts Bay until today. Despite its exceedingly long run, historians have pretty much ignored the modest Cape Cod, relegating it along with barns and mills to a sort of vernacular footnote. This photographic essay seeks to place this remarkable American house into historical context, as well as serve as a reminder of its special contribution to our patrimony.

Simple and straightforward, the Cape design has survived because it is so sensible. With their rectangular footprint and dearth of complicated offsets, the first examples were easily built. They required basic lumber and no foundations (sills were laid right on the Cape's sandy soil). The central chimney and boxy plan made them easy to heat. The roofs, composed of two slopes with no breaks or valleys, provided an extra half-story of space at less cost than constructing a full second level. The Cape was low—its main story had seven-foot ceilings. Held fast by its massive chimney, this compact shape allowed the house to ride out hurricanes, blizzards, and sand storms. There were no superfluous decorations—only what was necessary to shelter the inhabitants.

Whether because the floor plan was not flexible or because people wanted to preserve the attractive front, the house invariably grew toward the back. Eventually, these additions developed into a connected complex of house-shop-outbuilding-barn. That, too, was born of necessity, allowing farmers to reach barns and cattle without venturing into the Atlantic wind.

As in the child's sketch, the Cape Cod cottage says "house." While the classic Cape was indigenous to the sand dunes of southern New England—Yale president Timothy Dwight is credited with giving the cottage its name following a visit to Cape Cod in 1800—it gained acceptance across America. Maybe more important than its practicality, the Cape is a truly democratic form, a house for all people in this nation of immigrants.

The story of the Cape Cod cottage can be divided into two chapters. The "original" house that evolved from seventeenth-century English settlers' dwellings continued with only minor variations until the Civil War. Cape construction was then exceedingly rare for several decades, except in the most rural districts. In the 1920s a reborn Cape Cod became a staple ingredient of the colonial revival. The Cape's frugal plan and construction suited the lean times of the Depression, and by the 1950s, the Cape Cod style was firmly established as a mainstay of suburban development across the country. Now it remains to be seen if the scholarly recreations of early Capes, as well as contemporary versions of the Cape, will become a third chapter. To be sure, the early Capes are the most endearing—and rare. A tract house Cape from the 1950s may have less charm and patina than, say, a weathered 1750s New Hampshire farm Cape set in a pasture. Nevertheless, each Cape belongs on the same family tree.

Westport, Massachusetts, Waite-Potter house, 1677

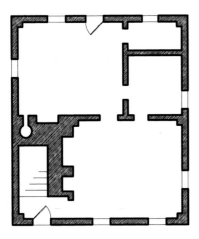

LEFT: Plan of a half Cape
RIGHT: Johnston, Rhode Island, Clemence-Irons house, 1691

*

The Mayflower landed at the far tip of Cape Cod, but the Pilgrims soon moved on in search of more abundant drinking water and less sandy soil. It was at Plymouth, on the western shore of the bay, where the earliest houses were built. Standing in for the earliest homes in New England, the reconstructed houses at the museum village of Plimoth Plantation show English domestic architecture transported to the New World.

Houses like those the settlers knew from the old country, suited to England's gentler climate, proved inadequate in the Massachusetts winter, so they soon abandoned exposed timbered walls and grass roofs for overlapping shingles. Surviving seventeenth-century houses are scarce and invariably heavily restored. Even so, the Jethro Coffin house on Nantucket (see page 30) illustrates the evolution of the Medieval English house into the American cottage. Large chimneys dominate these unusually substantial dwellings; the original plans have been expanded along the back face, creating the eponymous saltbox shape. Counterparts of these American houses, minus the shingled walls and roofs, once lined the narrow streets of many an Essex or Suffolk village. The fisherman's shacks of Siasconset Village on Nantucket offer similar recollections of their forebears in Devon and Cornwall.

Heredity is generally more important than environment in shaping people's tastes and their buildings styles. The earliest colonists in America built what they knew back home. So, while Swedes and Finns built log cabins along the Delaware River and the Dutch in the Hudson Valley built in brick, the English in southeastern New England originally built tall, narrow, half-timbered wooden houses that they roofed with thatch. Many Puritan housewrights brought their long tradition of carpentry skills from the wood building counties

CLOCKWISE FROM TOP LEFT: Setauket, Long Island, New York, Benjamin Thompson house; Eastham, Massachusetts, Higgins house, late 18th century; Truro, Massachusetts, John Mayo house

of East Anglia and from the west of England, but New England's harsh climate tested the pioneers' ingenuity. By lowering the house and pulling its plan into more of a square footprint, the transported English house evolved into the functional, wind-cheating house we call the Cape Cod cottage. Like most good utilitarian design, the simplicity of the early Cape was key to its two-hundred-year success.

Another reason for the longevity of the house type was the topography of Cape Cod itself—isolated from the mainland and resource poor. Many cottages were built in the colonies of Plymouth and in Massachusetts Bay, yet that sandy spit of land jutting seventy miles eastward into the ocean provided the best incubator and laboratory for the new cottage. Thus, the place and the house type became inextricably intertwined.

The peninsula we know as Cape Cod was discovered and named in 1602, but not a lot happened between then and President Dwight's travels there two centuries later. Settlers arrived from Plymouth in 1636, and they fished or farmed. The sea provided the only bounty, for the harvesting of trees for fuel and building eroded the once rich but thin topsoil. (By the time of Henry David Thoreau's visits in the early 1850s, the Cape's native oak was thoroughly depleted and lumber was being imported from Maine.) Until it became a tourist destination in the late nineteenth century, Cape Cod was a backwater. It lacked a deep harbor, so shipping was limited to fishing and coastal traffic; it did not have the fabulous fortunes that enriched so many New England ports, such as New Bedford, Nantucket, and Salem, where the domestic architecture was appropriately far more ambitious.

These fisherman and farmers dwelt, according to Dwight, in "thrifty though comfortable circumstances." Provincetown did not have a two-story house until 1820, and just about every house on the Lower Cape (from the elbow to the fist of the land's arm shape) was a characteristic cottage. Capes varied, but not by much. Elevations consisted of three, four, or five bays (half, three-quarter, and full Capes)—ranging from roughly twenty to forty feet in front elevation. The design grew from the plan, itself a direct descendant of the Elizabethan-period rural cottage. Whether it had one room or four, the cottage was built around a central chimney core that provided fireplaces to each room. The plan of the standard full Cape was almost square, being usually slightly wider across the front than it was deep. The layout consisted of small rectangular rooms, approximately one hundred to four hundred square feet each, with a large kitchen/workshop/family room to the rear. The upstairs sleeping space was reached by way of a miniscule entrance hall with steep stairs that hugged the chimney. There were no Renaissance-inspired ratios, and no proportional relationship more complicated than spacing windows besides the front door.

The construction of the Cape Cod cottage came easily to men experienced in erecting barns and building boats. Wide plank floors were laid on runners placed on the ground, while oak frames formed a strong skeleton of sills, corner posts, and roof plate. Vertical planks of a foot or more in width were nailed to the frame, and shingles were then nailed onto the planks (clapboards were occasionally used, but only on the front of the house).

To roof the house, planking was nailed on horizontal beams, called purlins that connected the triangulated trusses at the gable ends (there were no rafters or ridgepole). Echoing the heritage of thatching, long pine shingles, or shakes, were severely lapped on the roof, creating an impervious and easily repairable covering. An early Cape often appears to be mainly roof—the roof-to-front ratio was roughly sixty to forty. (Sometimes, the roof was raised into a double-pitched gambrel, but the acquisition of new space altered the classic form.)

Vertical pine boards, and later lath and plaster, formed the inside wall surface; the corner constructional supports were often exposed. Even with an added layer of paper or seaweed for insulation, a Cape's walls were no more than a few inches thick, which accounts for the protruding exterior window frames. Early Capes also have their window tops tucked right under the cornice.

Certain Capes, such as the Jabez Wilder house in Hingham (which may be as early as 1690), are noted for visibly curved "bow" roofs. The legend holds that shipwrights built bow roof houses in imitation of a ship's hull. Although the shape appears to be a unique local form, the bow is probably a memory of English cruck framing, that is,

CLOCKWISE FROM TOP LEFT: Lyme, New Hampshire, Enos Snow house, ca. 1790; Perkinsville, Vermont, Nathaniel Stoughton house, 1788; Lincolnville, Maine, De Bertrand farm; East Hiram, Maine, Daniel Small farm

CLOCKWISE FROM TOP LEFT: Norwichtown, Connecticut, Captain Richard
Charlton cottage, ca. 1800; Halifax, Massachusetts, Shadrach Standish
house; Charlton cottage, interior

CLOCKWISE FROM TOP LEFT: Rumford, Maine; Paine-Atkins House, Truro, Massachusetts, ca 1810–15 (photographed ca. 1890); Richmond, Maine

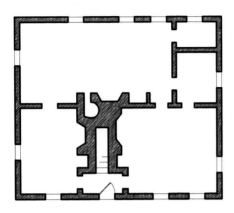

LEFT: Plan of a three-quarter Cape
BOTTOM: Livermore Falls, Maine

employing naturally bent trees in house building. The bowed roof arguably creates more space in the attic story, but the few inches of gained headroom hardly seem worth the trouble. Whether used for strengthening or as a sensual flourish, the bow adds a handsome but subtle element.

In the first pioneer houses, such as at Plymouth or the Clemence-Irons house in Johnston, Rhode Island (1691) the chimneys formed an end wall. Nevertheless, the functional wisdom of a central chimney won out; it also helped to stabilize the house, forming a mast about which the staircase was wrapped. The earliest chimneys were wood, but internal stacks of stone and brick replaced them as soon as was practical.

The Cape's most evocative architectural elements, the massive chimney and hearth-focused plan, were undone by advances in heating. The advent of the stove in the 1840s meant smaller chimneystacks and flues, and obviated the need for a central chimney. Flues for stoves could be placed anywhere in the plan, so families closed over the existing old fireplaces, while closets and stairs could be rearranged. The destruction of the proportional unity of the Cape Cod cottage cannot be underestimated, and it foreshadowed problems inherent in twentieth-century adaptations of the house. When viewed from straight on, the classic Cape's elevation is two-thirds roof.

The Cape also changed in other less drastic ways. Looking at the main facade, one can follow the lowering of the windows over time with wider spaces between eaves and window (fenestration was not an issue on the end walls). The old seven-foot ceiling height on the interior was not altered much, but in gaining some upstairs headroom, the front walls were raised to as much as ten feet. The proportion of roof-to-wall still overwhelmingly favored the roof.

The Cape did not lend itself to decorative flourishes, yet stylistic reflections of higher styles did appear. Tributes to the then-current Georgian or Federal styles are found primarily in the doorways. This could be as simple as reeded moldings flanking the door or relatively elaborate treatments complete with a pediment, pilasters, or an elliptical fanlight. The cottage and the Greek Revival worked surprisingly well together, as long as the Cape's proportional configuration was maintained.

Grecified Capes might have entrance porches with Ionic or Doric columns, but not porticos; there are even examples of cottages with both Greek and Gothic trim. Because the peaked end walls echoed a Greek temple form, many Capes—and their front entrances—were turned ninety degrees. But reorienting the house, and in many cases enlarging it, often upset the cottage's proportional purity.

When the front house was enlarged or a larger wing was attached, the earlier story-and-a-half cottage remained at the core. While Grecification and Gothicizing could be successful, the Cape's inherent completeness did not lend itself to upward expansion. It also resisted the addition of porches, columns, and other elements expressive of social mobility. The form was such a perfect solution to early settlers' requirements that even if an owner prospered, the proletarian Cape was just not suited to impressing the neighbors.

Originally a coastal form, the Cape adapted well to the uplands of Vermont and Maine, and it extended the reach and duration of the early form. As the forests were pushed back, the ubiquitous farmhouse of inland New England was the Cape. The tradition of the backwards-growing house—the ell that becomes extended back to the barn—was no better realized than in the connected farmsteads of Maine. Capes continued to be built in the New England hinterlands, but elsewhere the Cape Cod cottage had to wait for its renaissance in the colonial revival and in the post–World War II housing boom.

*

Cape Codders may have been too poor to knock down their cottages and replace them with the latest fashion, but the rest of the country witnessed an explosion of domestic styles in the second half of the 1800s. The Victorian era was overflowing with various popular architectural fashions. The Compagnie Française du Télégraphique de Paris à New York brought Second Empire mansard-roofed houses to Cape Cod, for example. The neoclassical styles lumped under the rubric of the beaux-arts enlivened the domestic landscape with verandahs, porticos, and all manner of colors and materials. Only the homegrown shingle style paid homage to vernacular New England dwellings, recalling the earlier shingled cottages of poor fishermen and hardscrabble farmers.

CLOCKWISE FROM TOP LEFT: Truro, Massachusetts, Ephraim Rich house, ca. 1830, triangulated gutter with drain hole; Eastham, Massachusetts, John Doane house; Montauk Point, New York, "Eothen," Rolf William Bauhan, architect, 1931–35; Wellfleet, Massachusetts, B. S. Young house, post-1843, full Greek revival treatment of a Cape

It is intriguing to think of the prairie style of Frank Lloyd Wright in the early 1900s as a collateral descendant of the American colonial home, including the Cape Cod cottage. Although Wright's plans were a direct assault on the box, his houses, like Capes, featured massive chimneys that served as the physical and spiritual center of the home. Both types hug the ground, there are no basements in either, and the second story is downplayed. In his Depression-era Usonian houses, Wright offered inexpensive housing that also echoed the democratic ideal of the early Cape. But it was the revival of American colonial styles, fostered by Wright's beaux-arts rivals, that fueled the nostalgia for Capes. Notable colonial revival examples were usually mansion-sized, but as an inspiration the historic Cape Cod cottage had the advantage of domestic scale and affordability—something that would be reinforced in the hard times and war years of the mid-twentieth century.

If one individual can claim credit for the renaissance of the Cape Cod cottage he is the Boston architect Royal Barry Wills (see page 78–79). Trained at MIT, he began his career in 1919, incidentally the same year that Walter Gropius began his influential tenure at the Bauhaus. Wills knew modern materials and designed his share of contemporary houses, but chose to devote himself to traditional New England homes, particularly the Cape. He was successful because he understood the soul and essence of the original cottage form, not least of all its proportional relationships. ("If they're kept simple the way they were intended to be, they're almost as modern as Modern.") His houses were not copies of early houses, yet he made "charm" an integral part of his formula—clients wanted a sense of home and hearth. They responded favorably to such features as garden gates and they welcomed the craftsmanship of oversized hand-wrought hinges—elements that modernists stripped from the American home. Wills produced hundreds of always-identifiable houses featuring the massive chimney and an authentic early Cape facade, while he stuck to his credo of no stock plans. In one of his many books, *Planning Your Home Wisely!* of 1946, he wrote, "I suppose the reason Cape Cod Houses are so popular is that they are the simplest expression of shelter."

In Wills's plans, fireplaces might even be more massive than their models, but the hearth was as much the heart of the creation as in Wright's Prairie houses. If a client wanted a larger house, the extra space was incorporated into the Cape Cod tradition of ells to the rear of the house. The plans could be quite variable—U-, L-, or H-shaped—but all of his houses maintained the one-and-a-half-story Cape front. A two-car garage that looked as though it was an early farm shed only recently and sympathetically converted to contemporary use could be attached .

While Wills is the best known, there were other champions of the Cape Cod cottage practicing across the country. For example, one similarly talented student of the early American house was Rolf William Bauhan. One of the first graduates of Princeton's architecture program, Bauhan worked on the restoration of Soissons Cathedral in northern France following its bombardment during World War I and was adept at creating English manor houses for wealthy exurbanites. His specialty, however, was the scholarly yet livable reinterpretation of the Cape; he designed hundreds of them, mostly in and around Princeton, New Jersey, but also on Cape Cod, eastern Long Island, and as far away as Puerto Rico.

Nevertheless, it was the immigrant modernists such as Marcel Breuer, Richard Neutra, and Mies van der Rohe who garnered fame as canonic house designers. Even the hoary Society for the Preservation of New England Antiquities took on Gropius's own 1936 house in Lincoln, Massachusetts as one of its museum properties. Although the architecture schools embraced modernism, the Cape was the preferred choice for those unable to afford a custom-built architect-designed house.

As a symbol of technological ingenuity and affordability, the Cape Cod is the domestic equivalent of the Model T Ford. Stock Cape Cod plans were extensively published in magazines and widely available in the 1930s, and there were even ready-built houses like the popular "Attleboro," a Cape produced by Sears. During the Depression, the seeming parsimony of the classic Cape boosted the style's national appeal, although the Cape also remained a symbol of putatively simpler days. The Cape, too, was more reassuring

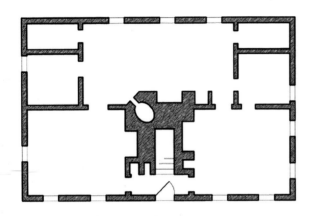

LEFT: Plan of a full Cape
BOTTOM: Louisville, Kentucky, Sears Cape "Attleboro,"
1950s

to mortgage lenders and builders hesitant to embrace new styles emanating from Europe via the architecture schools. The Cape Cod had become America's favorite house.

✳

The Cape Cod really came into its own following World War II. Modern architects produced new housing during the war, although it was often impermanent and as romantic as a Quonset hut. One exceptional wartime project was defense workers housing in Windsor Locks, Connecticut, in 1942 by Harvard instructor Hugh Stubbins. Despite vertical siding and a small chimneystack, there is Cape Cod heritage in the single-story twenty-six-foot-square two-bedroom boxes.

But perhaps one of the most intriguing houses to come out of the war was the Lustron, the brainstorm of Carl Strandlund, a manufacturer of porcelain enamel steel panels. Working from a former airplane factory in Ohio, Standlund produced almost twenty-five hundred of his revolutionary steel-framed houses between 1948 and 1950. The practical, easily assembled (only screwdrivers and wrenches needed), low-maintenance, single-story houses with gable roof looked like a futuristic Cape—and sprang from the same kind of Yankee ingenuity. The roof slope was gentler than the Cape, but the proportions were familiar and the house sat right on the ground. The Lustron was more in the spirit of the original than the many revival Capes that depended solely upon stylistic cues.

Gunnison Homes, another prefab housing manufacturer, produced a very successful inexpensive house that had a larger chimney (made of metal) and a vague feel of its seventeenth-century ancestor. Constructed of standardized waterproof plywood panels, each Gunnison house was trucked from the factory in New Albany, Indiana, to the owner's waiting concrete slab. Except for the steel casement windows, this unprepossessing and unrevolutionary looking Cape blended well with earlier neighbors. Gunnisons were shipped to over forty states; two dozen Gunnisons were built in a single neighborhood in Metheun, Massachusetts, in the early 1950s, while there are nearly three hundred Gunnisons in Lexington, Kentucky.

Windsor Locks, Connecticut, Defense Workers Housing, 1942, Hugh Stubbins, architect

The Cape's hegemony was truly established by Levittown, set in a former potato farm on Long Island. First-time homeowners wanted freestanding houses—no matter how small; they did not want city streets, row houses, or manifestations of European social-democratic housing theory. It was fashionable for architects and sociologists to dismiss Levittown as symptomatic of a faceless society, one lacking the rugged individualism of the pioneers who built the first Capes. Yet 17,000 houses were built at Levittown in the three years following the end of the war. Even if the new Cape seemed a long way from its forebear, Alfred Levitt, architect for Levitt & Sons, declared, "The Cape Cod was and still is the most efficient house ever developed in America." In the Levittown Cape, some of the common sense of the Cape survived: simple plan, gable roof, and one-and-a-half-story cube, without Tudor gables or expensive-to-build Georgian dormers.

Builders liked the box shape, which leant itself to factory-like assembly. The Federal Housing Authority had publicized

LEFT: Louisville, Kentucky, Lustron house, 1949
ABOVE: Levittown, New York, 1952

the Cape as a domestic ideal, thereby stamping its approval on the style as the most desirable house for Americans to build. True, most modern Capes were smaller than their forebears and their interior plans bore little resemblance to those of the original. Foundations and the FHA ceiling-height standard of eight feet further changed the critical proportions. The scale, subtlety, and charm of the early Cape were gone.

Nevertheless, the Levittown Cape and its imitators not only captured the essence of home, they remained about the cheapest way to build a house. Even more popular than the ranch house of the 1950s (itself a direct descendant of Wright's Prairie and Usonian houses), Capes were personalized with many adornments like porches, shutters, picture windows, and all kinds of siding, so that in real estate argot they became Colonial Capes, Mission Style Capes, Cape Cod Tudors, and no doubt Cape Ranches. Capes were thought of as "starter" houses and were unlikely to stay in the same family for several generations; whereas early settlers enlarged their Capes with ells, the modern Cape owner moved on to a larger (and presumably more stylistically pretentious) house.

The Cape Cod cottage had thus became the epitome of unadventurous, lowest common denominator design for the lower-middle class—and now that America had become a nation on wheels, a small house attached to a prominent garage. The architectural press of the time was pretty hard on the favored home choice of many Americans. In a story on the Cape Cod in *Architectural Forum* in 1949, the unidentified author wrote:

> It never occurs to the average man to question the validity of a prevailing style…the house is his front, his statement of respectability…he wants nothing freakish or extreme to set him apart from the accepted norm…in a chaotic world, the traditional house offered a sense of security.

He further quoted modernists George Nelson and Henry Wright, authors of *Tomorrow's House*, who called the Cape "a perfect mirror of a society most of whose members are desperately afraid of acting like independent individuals." Columbia University professor Talbot Hamlin was only slightly kinder: "Of all the thousand and one awful looking houses that are built for speculation, probably the Cape Cod is the least acutely painful."

The original Cape was an ingenious solution to a regional problem, a response to the landscape and impecunity. By the Eisenhower years hand building was long gone, and the Capes spreading across the entire East Coast and beyond had nothing to do with environmental considerations. After the war, the Cape became the most popular domestic design based on its looks, as well as the homey and nationalistic associations it triggered, particularly for returning GIs.

※

Such ideological comments seem rather quaint half a century later. The Cape Cod cottage may have been bastardized, but its appeal was unassailable. And the spirit of the Cape inspired some intriguing reappraisals. In New England, architects attempted to update regional tradition, producing sophisticated kit houses like Tech Built, Acorn, and Deck House, while adopting the prefab technology of Levitt and Lustron. More promising was the rediscovery of the past in the movement called postmodernism, in which architects took a new look at architectural history, reassessing styles that had been ignored or deprecated by their Bauhaus-trained teachers. The stylistic attic of the past suddenly was re-opened for plundering.

Amid the pilotis, appliquéd columns, and primary colors of the neo-Corbusians, the less elitist aspect of postmodernism advocated by Robert Venturi, Charles Moore, Robert Stern, and other inclusivist architects looked to the same styles that had inspired the colonial revivalists, such as the shingle style and the Cape Cod. The summerhouses and the old cottages of the New England coast were rediscovered, revered, and revived.

Venturi's iconic and revolutionary 1964 house for his mother in suburban Philadelphia shook up the architectural establishment. Yet its belt course, pedimental roofline, and massive chimney—and the economy of a story-and-a-half house sitting flat on the ground—say "house," an American home with roots in our past. And the pair of houses that Venturi and Denise Scott Brown designed on Nantucket comes close to the Cape ideal (see pages 84–86). Gone is the massive central chimney, and as summer homes they do not hunker down but stand up to take in the views. But the architects have eschewed superfluous ornament, and, most importantly, these Nantucket vacation houses recall the sense of setting that was so essential to the original Capes. These no-nonsense wooden boxes are not so far geographically or psychologically from the fishermen's cottages in Siasconset. The same can be said of the studio and house that Venturi built for two artists on Block Island: sensible rectangles economically sheathed in a shingled skin.

Other contemporary architects, particularly in New England, have been trying to recapture the feeling of the early Cape without copying it. Designers such as Jeremiah Eck, James Estes, and Graham Gund (see page 89) are seeking inspiration along the New England shore whence the style originated. Somewhat more crowd-pleasing are expensive and faithful recreations of early Capes; the Bow House, hand-built in Bolton, Massachusetts and shipped around the country, is perhaps the best example.

Who could doubt the endless attraction of the New England cottage when one reads of high-end developments in old England that stress early American styles and ambiance? The frame houses of Hamptons in Surrey look like refugees from a Shaker village, another utilitarian Yankee form. ("We're selling a dream," the sales director says.) Leybourne Lakes, in the Cotswolds, bless their model homes with such evocative names as Providence, Vermont, New Hampshire, and the very Capelike (but five-bedroom) Harvard. When asked about his new New England village's allure, the developer noted, "Stone and brick can be quite depressing. With the New England look you are immediately on holiday." We have come full circle in four hundred years.

Given the shoddy workmanship and environmental insensitivity of the mega-mansion, our current domestic craze, the traditional center-chimney home will look better with every passing year. The Cape Cod cottage may yet begin another generation.

*

The principle that makes the Cape Cod cottage as enduring a form as the best functional architecture may be that its success depends upon its lack of self-consciousness. The Cape is no more, no less than what it needs to be; it was born of necessity, and its integrity is compromised when expanded beyond its most important and immediate mission of shelter. It has been called a modern house, but perhaps it is also Zen in spirit.

At the time when the Pilgrims were settling Cape Cod, the Japanese were codifying architectural construction to insure the inclusion of religious and philosophical values. Modular and standard, but not identical, Japanese houses faced the sun, just as early Capes invariably faced south. Zen Buddhist monks in particular believed that humble dwellings were most indicative of spirituality—as part of the aesthetic of restraint, plain buildings constructed of plain materials expressed simplicity, art, and beauty.

Soetsu Yanagi, a Japanese cultural historian, noted the dearth of words in Western languages to describe something that is both profound and unassuming. "Can anything be more uncommon than the commonplace?" he asked in *The Unknown Craftsman*. In that book, Yanagi employed the tea ceremony to posit universal truths about beauty. The most prized tea utensils were "selected from the plain, the natural, the homely, the simple, and the normal," rather than the costly, the luxurious, and the over-decorated. When Yanagi saw the Kizaemon tea bowl, considered the world's finest, he was shocked by its ordinariness; a poor Korean peasant made it.

> It was not made with thoughts to display effects of detail, so there is no time for the disease of technological elaboration to creep in....It is not inspired by theories of beauty, so there is no occasion for it to be poisoned by over-awareness…it was created with a very simple purpose, so it shuns the world of brilliance and colour…the beauty is an inevitable outcome of that very ordinariness.

That, too, is the heart and soul of the Cape Cod cottage.

LEFT: Watch Hill, Rhode Island, "Wunnegin!" Bow House, 1989
RIGHT: Old Lyme, Connecticut, developer's Cape, 2005

PLATES

PREVIOUS PAGE: Edward Hopper's studio, Truro, Massachusetts
ABOVE: Jethro Coffin House, Nantucket, Massachusetts, 1686

Siasconset, Nantucket, Massachusetts, "Auld Lang Syne," 1675

ABOVE: Siasconset, Nantucket, Massachusetts, fishermen's cottages
OPPOSITE: Edgartown, Martha's Vineyard, Massachusetts, Vincent House, 1672

Vincent house, end detail

Vincent house, entrance detail

Vincent house, rear

Old Lyme, Connecticut, Justin Smith house, 1710

Smith house, exterior detail

Smith house, interior

Smith house, interior

Hopkins Mills, Rhode Island, Ezekiel Hopkins house, ca. 1720

Eastham, Massachusetts, Joshua Knowles house, 1741

Glocester, Rhode Island, Nathan Wade homestead, ca. 1751

Wade homestead, interior

ABOVE: Wells, Maine, Dorfield farm, built by Samuel Storer, pre-1762

LEFT: Shrewsbury, Massachusetts, Gershon Wheelock house, 1752 and Gideon Barlow house, 1827

Wesport, Maine, Greenleaf farm, ca. 1770

Arrowsic, Maine, Drummond house, ca. 1770–90

Mason, New Hampshire, Samuel Abbott house, 1773; boyhood home of Samuel Wilson, "Uncle Sam"

Jaffrey Center, New Hampshire, Johan Buchler (John Buckley) house, 1774; new wing, Richard Monahon, architect, 2004

Buchler House, exterior with 230 years of additions and alterations

55

LEFT: Harpswell Center, Maine, Tarr-Eaton house, ca. 1783
ABOVE: Union, Maine, Daggett house, ca. 1789

Daggett house

Daggett house

Nobleboro, Maine, Old Moody farmhouse, ca. 1790

Moody farmhouse

South Worthington, Massachusetts, Russell Conwell house, ca. 1790

Alna, Maine, farmhouse, 1798

Chilmark, Martha's Vineyard, Massachusetts, farm

Sesuit, Massachusetts, ca. 1790

Dublin, New Hampshire, Aimee Lamb house, 1837

Arnold Mills, Rhode Island, house ca. 1725; Greek facelift, 1837

Mills house, doorway detail

Provincetown, Massachusetts, ca. 1800–20

Groton, Connecticut, Captain Avery Brown house, ca. 1812

Harrisville, New Hampshire, C. C. P. Harris house, 1835

Thomaston, Maine, Lermond farm, 1820

Nantucket, Massachusetts, Greek Capes on Darling Street

Rockport, Maine, Greek Cape, ca. 1835

Rockport, Maine, Greek Cape, ca. 1840

Chatham, Massachusetts, Greek Cape, ca. 1850

LEFT: Harrisville, New Hampshire, "Peanut Row," workers housing, 1864
ABOVE: Westport, Massachusetts, Philip and Kate Cory Grinnell house, ca. 1890

Providence, Rhode Island, Royal Barry Wills house, ca. 1941–42

Wills house interior

Wellfleet, Massachusetts, summer cabins

Stone Harbor, New Jersey, seaside Cape, 1950s

Mattapoisett, Massachusetts, bow-roofed house, John Doran, architect, 1966

Nantucket, Massachusetts, Wislocki house, Venturi & Rauch, architects, 1970–72

Nantucket, Massachusetts, Trubek house, Venturi & Rauch, architects, 1970–72

Block Island, Rhode Island, Coxe and Hayden house and studio, Venturi & Rauch, architects, 1979–80

Coxe and Hayden house, detail

Nantucket, Massachusetts, guest house,
Graham Gund, architect, 1994

Southport, Maine, house collaged by Paul Bruno Mrozinski, architect, 1990, from Ely, Vermont barn and Webster, New Hampshire house, both ca. 1780

Chilmark, Martha's Vineyard, Massachusetts, Arbor house, Keith Moskow, architect, 2004

BIBLIOGRAPHY

Baisly, Claire, *Cape Cod Architecture*. Orleans, Mass.: Parnassus Imprints, 1989.

Briggs, Martin S., *The Homes of the Pilgrim Fathers in England and America*. New York: Oxford University Press, 1932.

"The Cape Cottage." In *Architectural Forum*, Part 1, February 1949; Part 2, March 1949.

Connally, Ernest Allen. "The Cape Cod House: An Introductory Study." In *Journal of the Society of Architectural Historians*, Vol. XIX, No. 2, May 1960.

Cummings, Abbott Lowell. *The Framed Houses of Massachusetts Bay 1625–1725*. Cambridge: Harvard University Press, 1979.

Doane, Doris. *A Book of Cape Cod Houses* (rev. ed.). Boston: David R. Godine, 2000.

Gitlin, Jane. *Updating Classic America: Capes*. Newtown, Conn.: Taunton Press, 2003.

Hubka, Thomas C. *Big House, Little House, Back House, Barn: The Connected Farm Buildings of New England*. Hanover, New Hampshire: University Press of New England, 1984.

Massey, James C. and Shirley Maxwell. *House Styles in America: The Old-House Journal Guide to the Architecture of the American Home*. New York: Penguin, 1996.

Maxwell, Shirley and James C. Massey. "From Dark Times to Dream Houses." In *Old-House Journal*, September/October 1999.

Morgan, William. "A Nearly Perfect House: Practical, Flexible, and Charming, the Cape Cod Cottage Endures as a Model of Home Design." In *The Boston Globe Magazine*, June 22, 2003.

Morrison, Hugh. *Early American Architecture*. New York: Oxford University Press, 1952.

Evelyn Nieves. "Wanted in Levittown: Just One Little Box With Ticky Tacky Intact." In the *New York Times*, Nov. 3, 1995.

Poor, Alfred Easton. *Colonial Architecture of Cape Cod, Nantucket and Martha's Vineyard*. New York: Dover, 1970 (reprint of 1932 book published by William Helburn, New York).

Royal Barry Wills Associates. *Houses for Good Living*. New York: Architectural Book Publishing, 1993.

Stanley Schuler. *The Cape Cod House: America's Most Popular Home*. Exton, Penna.: Schiffer Publishing, 1982.

Schuler, Stanley. *Saltbox and Cape Cod Houses*. Exton, Penna.: Schiffer Publishing, 1988.

"A Treasury of the Loveliest Homes Ever Published: Royal Barry Wills, F.A.I.A." In *The American Home*, October 1960.

Wilkinson, Jeff. "Who They Were: Royal Barry Wills." In *Old-House Journal*, July–August 1992.

PHOTOGRAPHY CREDITS

William L. Bauhan
18, lower right

Harvard Design School, Frances Loeb Library
19

Historic American Building Survey, Library of Congress:
8
9 (Arthur Haskell)
11, upper left
11, upper right (Arthur Haskell)
11, lower left (Cervin Robinson)
13, upper left (Aubrey P. Janion)
13, upper right
14, upper left (Jack Boucher)
14, bottom (Jack Boucher)
15, upper right
18, upper left (Cervin Robinson)
18, upper right (Cervin Robinson)
18, lower left (Cervin Robinson)

Maine Historic Preservation Commission:
13, lower right
13, lower left (George Codman)
15, upper left (Nyberg Studio)
16, lower right (A. N. Houdlette)
15, lower left (F. A. Wendell)

Carolyn Morgan:
22, right

Whitney Morrill:
10, left
16, top
20, top

All other photographs taken by the author 2004–2005